ULTIMATE COUPLES GUIDE TO A HEALTHY RELATIONSHIP

Navigating the Path to a Robust and Fulfilling Partnership-Your Comprehensive Companion to Relationship Well-being

<u>Cinthia T. Jones</u>

<u>Legal Notice</u>

TABLE OF CONTENT

INTRODUCTION

Welcome to the Ultimate Couples Guide To A Healthy Relationship, where we set out on a travel to investigate the fundamental components that contribute to a flourishing and persevering organization. In a world filled with differing challenges, keeping up a solid and important association together with your noteworthy other may be a significant interest.

This direct points to unwind the complex flow of effective connections, advertising bits of knowledge, down to earth exhortation, and demonstrated methodologies to cultivate communication, construct believe, and sustain the establishment of a adore that withstands the test of time. Connect us as we dive into the keys to passionate intimacy, effective strife determination, and the craftsmanship of developing shared objectives,

all woven together to form a embroidered artwork of persevering adore and fulfillment.

All through this travel, we are going explore the complexities of present day connections, recognizing that they advance and adjust over time. From the starting stages of captivation to the more profound, more nuanced angles of commitment, our direct will give you with the apparatuses to not as it were climate the inescapable storms but moreover to celebrate the sunny days of your shared life.

Communication lies at the heart of any flourishing relationship, and we are going investigate strategies to upgrade both verbal and non-verbal trades. Understanding each other's needs, effectively tuning in, and expressing feelings valuably are fair many of the abilities we'll dive into, fostering a association that goes beyond words.

Believe, another foundation of sound connections, will be dismembered to uncover its different aspects. We'll talk about building believe, keeping up it through challenges, and how a strong establishment of believe shapes the bedrock for a versatile association.

Exploring clashes smoothly is an unavoidable portion of any relationship. This direct will prepare you with strife determination techniques that advance understanding and strengthen the bond between you and your accomplice.

We'll investigate the significance of empathy, compromise, and finding common ground, guaranteeing that clashes ended up openings for development instead of deterrents.

As we move forward, we'll address the importance of shared objectives and values. From career desires to individual development and family arranging, adjusting your dreams and goals can make a sense of unity and purpose that supports your relationship through distinctive stages of life.

Eventually, this direct could be a compass for couples looking for not fair life span but honest to goodness fulfillment. Connect us as we embark on this travel to find the craftsmanship and science of cultivating a sound, flourishing, and persevering relationship.

Purpose of the Guide

The reason of the Extreme Couples Direct To A Sound Relationship is to empower individuals in sentimental partnerships with the information and aptitudes vital to develop and maintain a flourishing association. This direct points to:

Give Knowledge: Offer important bits of knowledge into the key components of a solid relationship, from viable communication and trust-building to struggle determination and shared objective setting.

Prepare with Viable Devices: Arm couples with commonsense instruments and procedures that can be executed in everyday life to improve their understanding of each other and fortify their passionate bond.

Navigate Challenges: Address common challenges confronted by couples, advertising direction on how to explore them usefully and change challenges into openings for development.

Advance Life span and Fulfillment:
Cultivate a profound understanding of the variables that contribute to the life span and fulfillment of a relationship, guaranteeing that couples not only endure challenges but also discover

delight and fulfillment in their shared travel.

Adjust to Alter: Recognize and adjust to the advancing nature of relationships, recognizing that development and change are fundamentally angles of a enduring organization. By satisfying these destinations, the guide aspires to be a valuable companion for couples at different stages of their travel, encouraging the advancement of flexible, concordant, and sincerely wealthy connections.

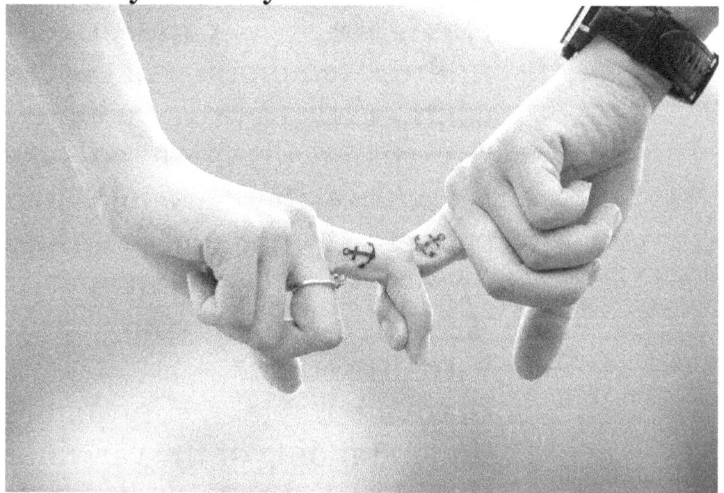

Importance of Healthy Relationships

The significance of solid connections expands distant past simple companionship, as they serve as the foundation of passionate well-being and individual advancement. Here are key reasons highlighting their noteworthiness:

Enthusiastic Bolster: Sound connections give a crucial source of passionate bolster. Having a partner who understands, empathizes, and stands by you amid both triumphs and challenges contributes to a sense of security and having a place.

Progressed Mental Wellbeing: Positive connections have been connected to progressed mental wellbeing. The enthusiastic association and companionship found in sound organizations can offer assistance reduce stretch, uneasiness, and sentiments of loneliness.

Enhanced Physical Wellbeing: Ponders appear that people in sound connections tend to involvement way better physical wellbeing. The passionate bolster and support given by a accomplice can emphatically affect generally well-being.

Expanded Strength: Confronting life's challenges is inescapable, but exploring them with a steady accomplice strengthens resilience. Healthy connections make a collaborative environment where accomplices can overcome deterrents together.

Individual Development: In a solid relationship, people are empowered to seek after individual development and self-discovery. The back and support from a accomplice can cultivate an environment where both people can flourish and accomplish their objectives.

Successful Communication Aptitudes: Connections flourish on viable communication. Sound associations teach individuals important aptitudes in communicating considerations, sentiments, and needs, advancing shared understanding and connection.

Positive Influence on Others: Sound connections serve as positive cases for others, whether it be companions, family, or the community. They contribute to a culture of compassion, participation, and regard, making a swell impact of positive social elements.

Life span and Fulfillment: Investigate demonstrates that people in fulfilling, long-term relationships tend to live longer and report higher levels of life fulfillment. The companionship and shared encounters contribute to a satisfying and important life.

Bolster in Accomplishing Goals: A strong accomplice can be a noteworthy resource in accomplishing individual and shared objectives. Whether it's seeking after a career, starting a family, or embarking on new enterprises, a sound relationship gives a establishment for common development.

In rundown, sound connections play a essential

part in advancing passionate well-being, cultivating individual advancement, and contributing to a more positive and strong society. Their affect amplifies into different perspectives of our lives, making the development and upkeep of such connections a beneficial and enhancing endeavor.

Chapter 1
Communication Skills

Successful communication is the soul of a sound relationship, serving as the bridge that interfaces people on a significant enthusiastic level. Here are key features of communication abilities pivotal for cultivating understanding and association:

Dynamic Tuning in: Developing the craftsmanship of dynamic tuning in is foremost. It includes not fair hearing words but completely locks in together with your partner's considerations and feelings, illustrating compassion and a honest to goodness want to get it.

Open and Genuine Expression: Energize open and legitimate expression of considerations and sentiments. Making a secure space where both accomplices feel comfortable sharing their vulnerabilities cultivates believe and develops enthusiastic closeness.

Clarity and Exactness: Endeavor for clarity and exactness in communication. Clearly communicating contemplations decreases the probability of mistaken assumptions, guaranteeing that messages are passed on precisely and eagerly are caught on.

Non-Verbal Communication: Pay consideration to non-verbal prompts such as body dialect and facial expressions. These inconspicuous signals regularly pass on feelings that words may not capture, including profundity to the understanding between accomplices.

Sympathy: Develop compassion, the capacity to get it and share in your partner's sentiments. Recognizing and approving your partner's feelings cultivates a sense of association and illustrates honest to goodness care.

Helpful Criticism: Give valuable input with affectability. Address concerns or clashes in a way that advances determination instead of protectiveness, emphasizing the collaborative nature of the relationship.

Timing and Tone: Be careful of the timing and tone of your communication. Choosing the correct minute and employing a conscious tone contribute to a positive climate, making talks more beneficial and less angry.

Struggle Determination Abilities: Learn and hone viable struggle determination abilities. This incorporates remaining focused on the issue at hand, dodging fault, and looking for commonly pleasant arrangements instead of emphasizing person triumphs.

Patience: Persistence is key, particularly when examining touchy themes. Permitting each other the time and space to precise contemplations and feelings guarantees that communication remains a helpful handle instead of a source of pressure.

Appreciation and Certification: Express appreciation and certification frequently. Recognizing your partner's positive qualities and endeavors strengthens a positive environment and reinforces the enthusiastic bond between you.

In pith, sharpening communication aptitudes is an progressing prepare that requires mindfulness, persistence, and a veritable commitment to understanding and being caught on. These aptitudes shape the establishment upon which a handful can construct a strong, flexible, and candidly wealthy relationship.

Successful communication may be a skill that can be sharpened through the hone of different strategies. Here are a few key procedures to enhance communication inside a relationship:

Dynamic Tuning in: Effectively lock in within the discussion by giving your full consideration to your accomplice. Listen without hindering, and reflect back what you've listened to guarantee understanding.

Utilize "I" Explanations: Outline your thoughts using "I" explanations to precise your sentiments and needs without placing blame. For case, say "I feel" rather than "You continuously."

Maintain a strategic distance from Presumptions: Clarify and inquire for clarification when required. Maintain a strategic distance from making presumptions around your partner's contemplations or sentiments, as this may lead to mistaken assumptions.

Non-Verbal Communication: Pay consideration to non-verbal signals such as body dialect and facial expressions. These signals frequently pass on feelings that will not be explicitly stated.

Select the Correct Time: Choose suitable times for discussions, particularly for delicate subjects. Timing can essentially affect the receptiveness of your accomplice and the generally viability of the communication.

Express Appreciation: Regularly express appreciation and appreciation. Recognizing your partner's positive actions reinforces the connection and energizes a positive communication environment.

Remain Calm: Keep up composure, particularly amid contradictions. Maintain a strategic distance from heightening conflicts by remaining calm and composed, permitting for a more levelheaded and beneficial talk.

Clarify Mistaken assumptions: In case errors emerge, look for clarification instead of making suspicions. Inquire open-ended questions to explore your partner's point of view and guarantee common understanding.

Utilize Positive Fortification: Reinforce positive behavior with positive criticism. Let your accomplice know when they've communicated successfully or when they've tended to your needs, cultivating a cycle of positive communication.

Compassion: Hone sympathy by putting yourself in your partner's shoes. Get it their point of view and approve their sentiments, indeed in case you do not fundamentally concur.

Dodge Cautious Reactions: When confronted with feedback, dodge getting to be protective. Instep, seek to get it your partner's concerns and work collaboratively towards a determination.

Center on Arrangements: Amid clashes, move the center from fault to finding solutions. Collaborate along with your accomplice to recognize noteworthy steps that can address concerns and make strides the situation.

By joining these successful communication strategies into your relationship, you create an environment where understanding, empathy, and shared regard prosper. These hones contribute to the overall health and versatility of your connection along with your partner.

Active Listening

Dynamic tuning in could be a foundational component of successful communication, cultivating understanding and association in connections. Here are key elements and methods associated with dynamic tuning in:

Grant Full Consideration: Illustrate your commitment to the discussion by giving your full consideration. Minimize distractions, put away electronic gadgets, and center on what your accomplice is saying.

Eye Contact: Maintain appropriate eye contact to communicate mindfulness and intrigued. Eye contact builds up a association and signals that you just are locked in within the discussion.

Non-Verbal Prompts: Utilize non-verbal cues, such as gesturing and facial expressions, to appear that you are effectively preparing and recognizing your partner's words. These signals fortify your nearness and understanding.

Dodge Interrupting: Resist the encourage to hinder or interject while your accomplice is talking. Permit them to precise themselves fully some time recently advertising your reaction, guaranteeing they feel heard and regarded.

Rewording and Summarize: Occasionally summarizing or summarize what your accomplice has said to confirm your understanding. This not only clarifies any potential mistaken assumptions but moreover consoles your accomplice that their message is being gotten precisely.

Inquire Clarifying Questions: Look for clarification by inquiring open-ended questions that empower your accomplice to elaborate on their contemplations and sentiments. This illustrates a veritable intrigued in understanding their perspective.

Reflect Emotions: Recognize and reflect the feelings your accomplice is communicating. For example, you might say, "It sounds like you feel baffled around..." This appears compassion and approves their enthusiastic experience.

Delay Judgment: Suspend judgment and maintain a strategic distance from shaping conclusions rashly. Let your accomplice express themselves completely some time recently shaping your reaction, cultivating an open and non-judgmental atmosphere.

React Fittingly: Once your accomplice has finished talking, react in a astute and obliging way. Share your contemplations and sentiments, illustrating that you've taken the time to process their point of view.

Express Empathy: Illustrate sympathy by communicating understanding and acknowledging your partner's sentiments. This makes a connection and fortifies the passionate bond between you. By effectively listening, you make a communication environment that advances shared understanding and fortifies the enthusiastic association in your relationship. This ability is essential for settling clashes, building believe, and cultivating a more profound sense of intimacy with your accomplice.

Conflict Resolution Strategies

Struggle could be a characteristic portion of any relationship, but how it is tended to and settled can essentially affect the generally wellbeing of the association. Here are compelling struggle determination procedures to explore differences and reinforce your relationship:

Remain Calm: Keep up enthusiastic composure amid clashes. Dodge raising pressures by remaining calm, collected, and centered on finding a determination instead of raising the difference.

Dynamic Tuning in: Effectively tune in to your partner's perspective without hindering. Get it their sentiments and concerns, and communicate that you just esteem their point of see.

Express Yourself Clearly: Clearly express your contemplations and sentiments utilizing "I" explanations. Dodge fault and center on communicating your feelings and needs in a way that advances understanding.

Look for to Get it: Endeavor to get it the fundamental issues and needs driving the strife. Inquire questions to pick up clarity and reveal the root causes of the contradiction.

Take a Break on the off chance that Required: In the event that feelings are running tall, it's affirm to require a break. Step absent from the circumstance incidentally to cool off and collect your contemplations. This will anticipate saying things in the warm of the minute which will be lamented afterward.

Utilize "We" Dialect: Outline discourses utilizing comprehensive dialect. Rather than "you vs. me," emphasize that you're working together as a group to discover a determination. This cultivates a collaborative approach.

Center on the Issue, Not the Individual: Keep the dialog centered on the particular issue at hand instead of making personal assaults. Dodge generalizing behavior and center on tending to the specific concern.

Brainstorm Arrangements Together: Collaboratively produce conceivable arrangements to the struggle. Conceptualizing energizes a sense of shared duty and can lead to creative ways to address the issue.

Compromise: Be open to finding middle ground. Both accomplices may ought to make concessions for a determination that fulfills both parties. Compromise may be a key component of effective strife determination.

Excuse and Let Go: Once a determination is come to, hone absolution and let go of waiting hatred. Holding onto feelings of resentment can weaken the positive determination and strain the relationship.

Set up Boundaries: Clearly communicate and set up boundaries that can help prevent recurring clashes. Understanding and regarding each other's boundaries contribute to a more advantageous energetic.

Look for Proficient Offer assistance in the event that Essential: In the event that conflicts persist or gotten to be as well challenging to resolve autonomously, consider looking for the help of a relationship counselor or advisor. Proficient direction can give extra experiences, communication apparatuses, and procedures custom-made to your particular relationship flow.

Keep in mind that struggle is an opportunity for development and understanding inside a relationship. By drawing closer differences with a valuable attitude and actualizing these strategies, you can change clashes into catalysts for fortifying the bond together with your accomplice and cultivating a more advantageous, more flexible relationship.

Chapter 2

Building Trust

Building believe may be a foundational component of any sound and enduring relationship. Here are key standards and methodologies for developing and keeping up believe along with your accomplice:

Open Communication: Cultivate open and straightforward communication. Share your considerations, sentiments, and encounters with trustworthiness, and energize your accomplice to do the same. Clear communication minimizes errors and builds a establishment of believe.

Consistency: Be reliable in your words and activities. Unwavering quality and consistency contribute to a sense of security, strengthening believe over time.

Take after Through on Commitments:

Honor your commitments and guarantees. Once you take after through on what you say you'll do, it builds up validity and unwavering quality, strengthening believe in your relationship.

Be Tried and true: Illustrate dependability by being there for your partner in times of require. Steady bolster amid both challenges and triumphs cultivates a sense of believe and dependence.

Apologize and Pardon: Recognize botches and apologize when necessary. Likewise, be open to excusing your accomplice. Solid connections recognize that everybody makes mistakes, and the capacity to apologize and pardon reinforces believe.

Set Boundaries and Regard Them: Clearly communicate and regard each other's boundaries. Establishing and honoring boundaries makes a sense of safety and security inside the relationship.

Appear Sympathy: Get it and approve your partner's sentiments. Illustrating compassion cultivates an passionate association, upgrading the generally trust between you.

Share Vulnerabilities: Permit yourself to be powerless with your accomplice. Sharing fears, insecurities, and desires builds a deeper enthusiastic association and strengthens believe.

Reliable Bolster: Offer reliable passionate back. Being a solid source of support and understanding during both challenging and blissful moments strengthens the bond of believe.

Straightforwardness: Be straightforward around your eagerly and activities. Dodge keeping insider facts or withholding data, as straightforwardness builds a establishment of believe and minimizes the potential for mistaken assumptions.

Prioritize Quality Time: Spend quality time together. Building believe isn't as it were almost verbal communication but also almost making shared encounters that develop your association.

Encourage Autonomy: Permit and bolster each other's person development and freedom. Believe thrives when accomplices feel certain in each other's capacity to navigate personal endeavors.

Building trust may be a ceaseless handle that requires time, consistency, and a shared commitment to the well-being of the relationship. By joining these standards into your intuitive, you contribute to the creation of a trusting and resilient establishment for your organization.

Trust-Building Exercises

Trust-building works out can be important instruments to enhance communication, foster emotional connection, and fortify the bond between partners. Here are a few works out that can contribute to building believe in your relationship:

Share Thanks: Take turns expressing specific things you

appreciate around each other. This work out empowers positive communication and strengthens the esteem you see in one another.

Powerlessness Challenge: Share individual stories or aspects of your life that make you feel powerless. This work out energizes openness and extends enthusiastic closeness.

Two-Way Road Journaling: Keep a shared journal where both accomplices compose almost their considerations, sentiments, and experiences. This ongoing discourse gives knowledge into each other's viewpoints and builds understanding.

Communication Workshop: Lock in in a communication workshop or seminar together. Learning and practicing effective communication skills can fortify the establishment of believe in your relationship.

Trust-Building Questions: Ask each other intentional and intelligent questions planned to develop your understanding of each other's values, yearnings, and fears. Illustrations incorporate "What does believe cruel to you?" or "How can I superior back you?"

Collaborative Objective Setting:

Work together to set short-term and long-term goals for your relationship. This collaborative process builds a sense of shared reason and commitment.

Mindfulness Reflection:

Hone mindfulness meditation together. This may advance enthusiastic mindfulness, decrease stretch, and make a calm and steady environment.

Shared Decision-Making:

Lock in in decision-making forms together, whether it's arranging a excursion, choosing home stylistic layout, or making financial decisions. This collaborative approach fortifies shared believe and regard.

Trust Falls: Whereas a classic work out, believe falls can be adjusted to construct passionate believe. Discuss fears, uncertainties, or personal challenges, and after that allegorically "drop" into each other's bolster and understanding.

Appreciation Letters: Write letters expressing gratitude and appreciation for your accomplice. Share these letters with each other, emphasizing specific qualities or activities that contribute to your sense of believe.

Struggle Determination Reenactment: Role-play speculative clashes and hone settling them together. This work out permits you to create and refine conflict resolution aptitudes in a low-stakes environment.

Arbitrary Acts of Benevolence: Astonish each other with mindful signals or acts of benevolence. These little, unexpected actions construct a sense of unwavering quality and thought, contributing to trust. Keep in mind, the adequacy of these works out lies within the commitment of both partners to effectively participate and lock in with an open heart and intellect. Steady hone of trust-building exercises can make a more versatile and associated relationship over time.

Honesty and Transparency

Honesty and straightforwardness are essential columns of a solid relationship. Here are key principles and techniques to develop and keep up these qualities:

Open Communication: Foster an environment where open and genuine communication is valued. Encourage your accomplice to precise their considerations and sentiments without fear of judgment.

Share Your Feelings: Be willing to share your feelings, concerns, and vulnerabilities with your accomplice. Genuine expression of feelings fosters a more profound understanding and association.

Be Honest: Hone trustworthiness in all angles of your relationship. Dodge stowing away data or making a untrue narrative. Trust is built on a establishment of honesty.

Concede Botches: Recognize your botches and take duty for them. Being honest about your mistakes and learning from them strengthens trust and illustrates individual development.

Dodge Duplicity: Steer clear of double dealing or half-truths. Complete transparency builds a sense of security and consoles your accomplice that they can depend on your keenness.

Reliable Behavior: Endeavor for consistency in your words and activities. Illustrating unwavering quality and consistency builds trust over time.

Discuss Expectations: Have open discussions almost desires with respect to trustworthiness and straightforwardness within the relationship. Clarify what each accomplice considers acceptable and work towards common understanding.

Handle Difficult Conversations: Approach difficult discussions with trustworthiness and sensitivity. Being frank almost challenging subjects, whereas keeping up regard, contributes to a more advantageous determination.

Look for Feedback: Encourage your partner to provide feedback on how you'll be able be more transparent or communicative. A eagerness to get input appears a commitment to development and enhancement.

Share Decision-Making: Include your partner in decision-making processes. Straightforwardness in choices strengthens the thought that you just esteem their input and need to construct a shared future.

Clarify Eagerly: Clearly communicate your intentions and motives. When your accomplice gets it your perspective and inspirations, it advances believe in your activities.

Be Open Almost Changes:

If there are changes in your life, whether individual or proficient, be open approximately them. Straightforwardness amid times of alter builds believe by keeping your accomplice educated.

By prioritizing trustworthiness and straightforwardness, you make a foundation of believe that's pivotal for the life span and well-being of your relationship. These qualities not as it were reinforce the association between partners but also contribute to a sense of security and emotional intimacy.

Establishing Boundaries

Laying out clear and solid limits is fundamental for keeping up with equilibrium, regard, and prosperity inside a relationship. Here are key standards and methodologies for really laying out and keeping up with limits:

Self-Reflection: Find opportunity to consider your own requirements, values, and individual cutoff points. Understanding yourself is the most vital phase in laying out limits that line up with your prosperity.

Open Correspondence: Examine limits straightforwardly and sincerely with your accomplice. Make a place of refuge for both of you to communicate your necessities, assumptions, and solace levels.

Shared Arrangement: Lay out limits through common understanding. The two accomplices must effectively take part in defining limits to guarantee they are fair and consensual.

Regard Each Other's Independence: Respect and acknowledge each other's autonomy. Solid limits consider individual development and individual space inside the setting of the relationship.

Be Explicit: Obviously characterize your limits, making them explicit and concrete. Vagueness can prompt false impressions, so understandable your assumptions with clearness.

Console Love and Responsibility: Stress that defining limits isn't an impression of an absence of affection or responsibility. About establishing a strong climate regards each accomplice's singular necessities.

Change on a case by case basis: Comprehend that limits might advance over the long run. Be available to reconsidering and changing limits in light of changes in conditions, self-improvement, or changes in the relationship elements.

Consistency: Be steady in maintaining the laid out limits. Consistency supports trust and assists the two accomplices with having a good sense of safety inside the relationship.

Express Limits Decidedly: Outline your limits in a positive light. Rather than zeroing in on limitations, underline how these limits add to the wellbeing and maintainability of the relationship.

Be Decisive, Not Forceful: Self-assuredly impart your limits without animosity. Use "I" explanations to communicate your necessities and assumptions such that cultivates seeing as opposed to protectiveness.

Comprehend and Acknowledge Contrasts: Perceive that every individual might have different solace levels and needs with regards to limits. Be understanding and tolerating of these distinctions, settling on something worth agreeing on where conceivable.

Ordinary Registrations: Plan customary registrations to talk about how the laid out limits are functioning for the two accomplices. This continuous exchange guarantees that the limits stay applicable and viable.

Keep in mind that maintaining healthy boundaries helps a relationship feel safe and secure. They make a structure for deferential and kind communication, permitting the two accomplices to flourish independently and as a Couples.

Chapter 3

Quality Time Together

Quality time together is a foundation of a solid and satisfying relationship. Here are key standards and methodologies to upgrade the nature of time enjoyed with your accomplice:

Focus on Presence: Focus on being completely present when you're together. Limit interruptions, for example, telephones or business related matters to boost the nature of your cooperation.

Plan activities that matter: Take part in

exercises that hold importance for both of you. Whether it's investigating shared side interests, attempting new encounters, or returning to most loved places, significant exercises fortify your association.

Make Ceremonies: Lay out ceremonies or schedules that are one of a kind to your relationship. Whether it's a week by week film night, a month to month experience, or an everyday registration, these ceremonies give a feeling of congruity and expectation.

Open Correspondence: Utilize your quality opportunity to participate in open and significant discussions. Talk about your yearnings, share your considerations and sentiments, and effectively pay attention to your accomplice's point of view.

Assortment in Cooperations: Vary the kinds of things you do together. To keep the relationship alive and exciting, strike a balance between quiet, intimate moments and experiences that are more dynamic and adventurous.

Shock Signals: Imbue immediacy into your relationship with shock signals. Whether it's an unexpected date, a manually written note, or a little smart gift, shocks add a component of euphoria and sentiment.

Higher expectations without ever compromising: Prioritize quality over quantity when spending time together. When compared to prolonged periods of time spent together without engaging in conversation, focused, meaningful interactions can have a greater impact on your connection.

Goals We Share: Pursue shared objectives as a team. This could mean making plans for the future, setting goals together, or even starting projects together. Shared objectives make a feeling of solidarity and reason.

Appreciation Articulations: Routinely express appreciation for your accomplice. Recognize their endeavors, characteristics, and the positive effect they have on your life. Veritable appreciation fortifies the close to home bond.

Together, unplug: Spend time away from social media and electronic devices. This permits you to interface all the more genuinely with one another without outside interruptions.

Learn Together: Investigate new interests or obtain new abilities together. Whether it's taking a class, going to studios, or learning another side interest, shared opportunities for growth extend your association.

Quality Time versus Routine Time: Make a distinction between quality time and routine time. While routine exercises are essential, guarantee that you likewise put away purposeful minutes for quality collaborations that support your close to home association.

By consolidating these standards and systems, you can enhance the nature of time enjoyed with your accomplice, encouraging a more profound association and making enduring recollections in your relationship.

Meaningful Activities

Participating in significant exercises reinforces the close to home association between accomplices. Here are different and significant exercises to consider for quality time together:

Cooking Together: Team up in the kitchen to set up an extraordinary feast. A common movement consolidates imagination and the delight of partaking in a delectable feast together.

Outside Undertakings: Set out on open air undertakings like climbing, trekking, or an end of the week escape. Nature has an approach to cultivating association and making noteworthy encounters.

Voluntary Service: Take part in volunteer exercises or altruistic work together. A shared cause can strengthen your bond and give you a sense of purpose.

Creative Pursuits: Together, take up artistic pursuits like painting, pottery, or taking art classes. Creativity is boosted and self-expression is encouraged when we work together to create something.

Reading Group for Two: Peruse a similar book and examine it together. The opportunity for intellectual engagement and thoughtful discussions is provided by this shared literary experience.

Stargazing: Go through a night stargazing. Whether it's in your patio or at a close by observatory, it's a tranquil and heartfelt method for associating while at the same time wondering about the universe.

Adventures in Travel: Plan an end of the week escape or a drawn out get-away to an objective you both longing. Making new memories with your friends is priceless.

Puzzles or games for boards: Play prepackaged games or work on puzzles as a team. It's a tomfoolery and intelligent method for hanging out, cultivating cooperation and cordial rivalry.

Wellness Together: Join a wellness class or take part in proactive tasks together, whether it's running, cycling, or rehearsing yoga. Not only is exercise good for your health, but it also gives you a chance to work together to achieve goals.

Photography Investigation: Go for a photography stroll together. Catch minutes, view, or anything that gets your attention. It's an innovative method for reporting your time and make a common visual journal.

Go to Studios or Classes: Sign up for studios or classes that interest both of you, whether it's moving, cooking, or learning another dialect. Shared opportunities for growth can be both pleasant and instructive.

Tour of Memory Lane: Go on an outing through a world of fond memories by returning to huge spots in your relationship. It very well may be where you initially met, had your most memorable date, or any spot that holds nostalgic worth.

Keep in mind, the way to significant exercises is the common happiness and association they bring to your relationship. Pick exercises that resound with both of you and line up with your inclinations, setting out open doors for shared happiness and development.

Nurturing Emotional Connection

Sustaining profound association is indispensable for a solid and satisfying relationship. The following are methods for strengthening the emotional connection between partners:

Offer Thanks: Show your partner how much you value their qualities, actions, and the positive influence they have on your life on a regular basis. Appreciation supports the close to home association.

Quality Discussions: Take part in significant and open discussions. Examine your contemplations, sentiments, and goals, encouraging a more profound comprehension of one another.

Undivided attention: Practice undivided attention during discussions. Give your partner your full attention, respond thoughtfully to what they say, and show empathy.

Share Weaknesses: Permit yourself to be open to your accomplice. Share your feelings of trepidation, dreams, and frailties, making a space for profound closeness.

Make Customs of Association: Lay out ceremonies that upgrade your profound association, like an everyday registration, an extraordinary sleep time schedule, or week after week date evenings.

Shock Signals: Imbue immediacy into your relationship with shock motions. Little thoughtful gestures or astonishments show mindfulness and fortify profound bonds.

Make Shared Objectives: Cooperate to define and accomplish shared objectives. Whether they're present moment or long haul, shared yearnings add to a feeling of solidarity.

Actual Love: Focus on actual fondness. Embraces, kisses, and actual touch discharge oxytocin, advancing sensations of association and holding.

Have fun together: Track down open doors for giggling and shared happiness. Whether through watching an interesting film or getting a charge out of cheerful exercises, chuckling upgrades close to home association.

Support During Difficulties: Be a wellspring of help during testing times.

Offering profound help exhibits your responsibility and fortifies your association.

Recognize Accomplishments: Commend each other's accomplishments and triumphs. Recognizing achievements encourages a positive and steady profound climate.

Apologize and Excuse: When necessary, apologize, and practice forgiveness. Tolerating each other's flaws and gaining from botches adds to a really lenient and associated relationship.

Think back About Certain Recollections: Carve out opportunity to think back about certain recollections you've shared. Considering blissful minutes builds up the positive parts of your relationship.

Plan Future Experiences: Talk about and plan future experiences or achievements. Expecting shared encounters makes a feeling of fervor and supports your close to home association.

Embrace Change Together: Embrace development and change as a team. Support each other's self-awareness and explore life's changes as a unified group.

By effectively integrating these techniques into your relationship, you can support and reinforce the close to home association with your accomplice, cultivating a more profound, stronger bond.

Adjusting Freedom and Fellowship

Adjusting freedom and harmony is vital for keeping a sound and supportable relationship. Here are techniques to track down the right harmony among distinction and shared encounters:

Open Correspondence: Talk about your requirement for autonomy and fellowship straightforwardly with your accomplice. The foundation for finding a strategy that works for both of you is having an understanding of each other's preferences.

Characterize Individual Limits: Set and communicate your personal boundaries in a clear way. This incorporates individual requirements for alone time, individual space, and independence in navigation.

Keep up with Individual Side interests: Keep seeking after individual leisure activities and interests. Having special goals cultivates a feeling of satisfaction and permits each accomplice to keep areas of strength for an of self.

Plan Alone Time: Put away devoted alone time for each accomplice. It is essential to make time for one's own personal reflection and rejuvenation, whether it be during a private outing or a quiet evening at home.

Empower Self-improvement: Support and energize each other's self-improvement and advancement. This may entail independently pursuing educational, professional, or personal goals.

Shared Objectives and Exercises: Distinguish shared objectives and exercises that line up with the two accomplices' inclinations. Settling on something worth agreeing on improves harmony without compromising distinction.

Customary Registrations: Plan standard registrations to examine how each accomplice is feeling about the harmony among autonomy and fellowship. This continuous discourse keeps up with arrangement.

Regard Each Other's Decisions: Regard each other's decisions and choices. Confiding in your accomplice to pursue free decisions supports a feeling of independence inside the relationship.

Observe Contrasts: Praise the distinctions among you and your accomplice. A relationship becomes richer and more diverse when people embrace their individuality.

Lay Several Ceremonies: Make ceremonies that cultivate fellowship, like a week after week film night, a month to month exposing, or an extraordinary end of the week schedule. These customs give devoted chance to shared encounters.

Share Liabilities: Appropriate liabilities and tasks fairly. While allowing for individual time off, a shared sense of responsibility fosters teamwork.

Focus on Taking care of oneself: Make it clear that both partners need to take care of themselves. Support exercises that advance mental, close to home, and actual prosperity autonomously.

Be Adaptable: Perceive that the harmony among autonomy and fellowship might move over the long run. Be adaptable and versatile to the changing requirements of each accomplice and the relationship.

Establish a Steady Climate: Encourage a strong climate where each accomplice feels open to communicating their requirements and wants. This aides in exploring the sensitive harmony among freedom and fellowship.

By carrying out these techniques, couples can make a dynamic and agreeable harmony between keeping up with individual personalities and encouraging a profound association with one another. Finding the right balance adds to the general wellbeing and life span of the relationship.

Chapter 4

Managing Challenges

Managing Obstacles In order to keep a relationship strong and thriving, one of its most important aspects is successfully overcoming obstacles. Here are methodologies to explore hardships and reinforce your association during testing times:

Open Correspondence: Lay out a groundwork of transparent correspondence. Encourage your partner to do the same by expressing your feelings, worries, and thoughts to them.

Undivided attention: Practice undivided attention during testing discussions. Guarantee that you completely comprehend your accomplice's viewpoint prior to answering, cultivating understanding and compassion.

Group Approach: Move toward difficulties collectively. Team up with your accomplice to find arrangements and face hardships together as opposed to finding fault or survey issues as individual issues.

Keep up With deference: Keep a deferential tone and disposition in any event, while examining testing themes. Treat your join forces with a similar politeness and thought you would anticipate.

Look for Arrangements, Not Fault: Center around finding arrangements instead of allotting fault. A critical thinking approach encourages a feeling of collaboration and participation.

Set Practical Assumptions: Lay out reasonable assumptions for one another and the relationship. Unreasonable assumptions can prompt dissatisfaction and disappointment.

Focus on Taking care of oneself: Deal with your own prosperity during testing times. Guaranteeing you are intellectually and sincerely solid permits you to contribute emphatically to the relationship.

Gain from Difficulties: View difficulties as any open doors for development and learning. Consider the examples you can separate from tough spots to fortify the relationship.

Advising or Treatment: Think about looking for proficient assistance in the event that difficulties persevere. Relationship advising or treatment can give direction and devices to explore complex issues.

Apologize and Excuse: Apologize when vital and practice pardoning. Relinquishing disdain and excusing your accomplice adds to recuperating and pushing ahead.

Lay out Limits: Obviously convey and regard each other's limits, particularly during testing times. Limits give a structure to exploring troubles with common comprehension.

Flexibility: Be adaptable and versatile in your way to deal with difficulties. Life is dynamic, and the capacity to conform to changing conditions is fundamental for a versatile relationship.

Observe Victories: Recognize and celebrate little triumphs and victories, regardless of how minor. Positive experiences contribute to a more upbeat outlook.

Express Sympathy: Show sympathy and understanding towards your accomplice's encounters and sentiments. This forms an association and builds up basic reassurance during challenges.

Remain Committed: Reaffirm your obligation to the relationship during difficult stretches. A solid feeling of responsibility helps weather conditions difficulties and encourages a conviction that all is good.

Recall that confronting difficulties together can fortify your bond and add to the general development of your relationship. By utilizing these methodologies, you can explore hardships all the more really and arise with a more profound association.

Overcoming Relationship Obstacles

Defeating relationship deterrents requires a blend of figuring out, correspondence, and joint exertion. Here are methodologies to explore and beat normal difficulties:

Distinguish Underlying drivers: Cooperate to distinguish the underlying drivers of the obstructions you're confronting. Understanding the hidden issues is essential for tracking down compelling arrangements.

Transparent Correspondence: Encourage transparent correspondence. Examine your sentiments, concerns, and points of view in a valuable way, making a place of refuge for the two accomplices to articulate their thoughts.

Stay away from Fault: Rather than accusing one another, emphasis on the main thing in need of attention. Use "I" proclamations to communicate your sentiments and requirements without relegating fault, cultivating a cooperative critical thinking approach.

Look for Understanding: Endeavor to figure out your accomplice's point of view. Undivided attention and sympathy assist with building an underpinning of common figuring out, in any event, when confronted with contrasting perspectives.

Cooperative Critical thinking: Move toward obstructions collectively. Team up to track down arrangements that the two accomplices can settle on, building up the possibility that you're cooperating to conquer difficulties.

Concentrate on Solutions: Concentrate on possible solutions rather than the issue at hand. Conceptualize together and focus on finding a way noteworthy ways to address the difficulties you're confronting.

Gain from Past Difficulties: Think about past difficulties and the methodologies that were effective in conquering them.

Apply illustrations figured out how to successfully explore current impediments more.

Show restraint: Beating hindrances frequently takes time. As you work toward a solution, be patient with the process and each other.

Compromise: Be available to think twice about. Finding center ground frequently includes the two accomplices making concessions to help the relationship.

Look for Proficient Direction: In the event that important, think about looking for the help of a relationship guide or specialist. Proficient direction can give extra devices and experiences to conquering explicit difficulties.

Customary Registrations: Plan customary registrations to evaluate progress and talk about any continuous difficulties. Continuous correspondence keeps issues from raising.

Develop Strength: Foster strength as a team.

Comprehend that difficulties are a characteristic piece of any relationship, and your capacity to return and become together is vital.

Observe Progress: Recognize and celebrate progress, regardless of how little. Perceiving accomplishments, regardless of how gradual, builds up forward movement.

Reconnect Inwardly: Make deliberate efforts to emotionally reconnect. Get to know each other, express love and appreciation, and sustain the close to home connection between you.

Excuse and Let Go: Practice absolution and let go of past complaints. Clutching disdain can block progress and keep the relationship from pushing ahead.

By moving toward snags with a cooperative outlook, responsibility, and powerful correspondence, couples can defeat difficulties and arise with a more grounded, stronger relationship.

It is essential to manage stress and external pressures to keep a healthy relationship. Here are techniques to explore outside difficulties and keep major areas of strength for a:

Bound together Front: Move toward outside pressures collectively. Present a unified front, building up the possibility that you both face difficulties together and support one another.

Communicating openly: Impart transparently about outer stressors. Share your interests, pay attention to your accomplice's point of view, and work together to track down arrangements.

Lay out Needs: Obviously characterize your needs as a team. Making decisions that are in line with your shared goals and values is made easier when you know what matters most.

Expectations that are attainable:
Be sensible about what you can deal with. Set attainable

assumptions for both yourselves and the relationship, taking into account outer requests.

Management of Time: Foster compelling time usage techniques. To avoid feeling overwhelmed, set aside time for one another, self-care, and shared responsibilities.

Make an Emotionally supportive network: Establish a network of friends, family, or a support group as a source of assistance. Having outer help can facilitate the weight during testing times.

Normal Registrations: Plan customary registrations to examine how outside pressures are influencing both of you. This continuous exchange guarantees that you're mindful of one another's encounters and can offer help on a case by case basis.

Practice Pressure Alleviation Strategies: Include

strategies for reducing stress in your daily routine. Whether it's activity, care, or side interests, finding sound source for pressure can decidedly influence your relationship.

Keep up with Limits: To shield your relationship from excessive external pressures, establish and uphold boundaries. Figure out how to say no when important to protect your significant investment.

Delegate Liabilities: On the off chance that conceivable, agent or offer liabilities. Disseminating undertakings can keep one accomplice from feeling overpowered and advance a feeling of cooperation.

Recognize Small Successes: Even in the midst of difficulties, recognize and celebrate the smallest achievements. Positive mentality is fostered by recognizing progress.

Adaptable Critical thinking: Be adaptable in critical thinking. Outside tensions might require adjusting plans or systems, and an adaptable methodology can make the interaction smoother.

Quality Time: Focus on quality time together. In any event, during unpleasant periods, tracking down minutes to associate and unwind builds up your profound bond.

Keep up with Individual Prosperity: Deal with your singular prosperity. Guaranteeing that the two accomplices are intellectually and sincerely sound adds to the general strength of the relationship.

Adjust to Change: Perceive that outer tensions might carry changes to your everyday practice or plans. Couples who are flexible and open to change have an easier time navigating difficult times.

By executing these techniques, couples can explore outside pressures with versatility and keep major areas of strength for a, even despite stressors.

Long-Term Relationship Maintenance

Long haul relationship upkeep includes continuous endeavors to support, reinforce, and adjust the relationship over the long haul. Here are systems to support a sound and satisfying long haul relationship:

Normal Registrations: Make time for regular check-ins to talk about how your relationship is doing. This gives a valuable chance to address concerns, express necessities, and guarantee you both feel appreciated.

Quality Time: Keep on focusing on quality time together. As life develops, keeping major areas of strength for a requires deliberate endeavors to share significant encounters.

Shared Objectives and Dreams: Return to and update shared objectives and dreams. This guarantees that you're both moving toward a path that lines up with your yearnings as a team.

Individual Development: Encourage one another's personal development and growth. Support chasing after new interests, training, and expert undertakings.

Adaptability: Be willing to change your relationship and personal circumstances. Adaptability considers the development of your association as conditions change.

Observe Achievements: Celebrate relationship achievements and commemorations. Commitment is reaffirmed and happy memories are made when you acknowledge the time you spent together.

Show your appreciation: Routinely express appreciation for your accomplice. Little tokens of appreciation add to a positive climate and build up the worth you put on one another.

Keep Sentiment Alive: Keep on imbuing sentiment into your relationship. Shock one another, plan date evenings, and keep a feeling of energy.

Correspondence Improvement: Put resources into relational abilities. As your relationship develops, refining your capacity to impart actually turns out to be progressively significant.

Reignite Energy: Investigate ways of reigniting energy and closeness. This might include attempting new things in the room, communicating wants, or looking for direction from experts if necessary.

Travel Together: If conceivable, keep on voyaging together. Investigating new spots and making shared recollections can revive your association.

Guiding or Studios: Consider going to relationship directing or studios occasionally. Proficient direction can give new points of view and instruments to improve your association.

Keep up with Shared Regard: Maintain mutual respect. Treat your join forces with the very thought and consideration that you did in the beginning phases of your relationship.

Explore Difficulties collectively: Move toward difficulties collectively. The more extended a relationship endures, the more probable you'll confront different hindrances. When you face challenges together, you strengthen your bond.

Family Arranging Conversations: On the off chance that material, participate in open conversations about family arranging. This incorporates contemplations about youngsters, vocation changes, and other significant choices.

Cultivate Fellowship: Make friendship a priority in your relationship. A solid underpinning of companionship is necessary to supporting a drawn out heartfelt association.

Keep Finding out About One another: Individuals develop over the long run. Try to keep finding out about one another's evolving inclinations, objectives, and yearnings.

Focus on Profound Closeness: Profound closeness is all around as significant as actual closeness. Focus on sharing sentiments, considerations, and weaknesses to keep a profound close to home association.

By coordinating these methodologies into your relationship, you add to the continuous development and imperativeness of your drawn out association. Consistently rethinking and adjusting these methodologies guarantees that your relationship remains satisfying and tough throughout the long term.

Chapter 5
Emotional Intimacy

Close to home closeness is the profound association and understanding divided among accomplices. Here are techniques to develop and improve close to home closeness in your relationship:

Open Correspondence: Cultivate transparent correspondence. Share your contemplations, sentiments, and encounters straightforwardly, making a space for weakness and understanding.

Undivided attention: Make sure you listen actively. Offer your accomplice your full consideration, pose explaining inquiries, and show compassion to understand their point of view completely.

Show your appreciation: Consistently express appreciation for your accomplice. Recognize their characteristics, endeavors, and the positive effect they have on your life.

Share Individual Stories: Share personal experiences and stories. Focusing on your over a significant time span constructs a more profound comprehension of one another's excursion.

Dedicated Time: Spend quality time together first. Take part in exercises that advance association, whether it's a tranquil night at home or a significant trip.

Common Help: Deal and look for everyday encouragement. Show up for one another during both testing and euphoric minutes, supporting that you are a solid wellspring of solace.

Establish Connection Rituals: Lay out customs that advance association, like day to day registrations, shared leisure activities, or end of the week customs. Reliable ceremonies improve profound closeness.

Express Love and Fondness: Verbally express your adoration and fondness. Customary confirmations of adoration reinforce the profound connection between accomplices.

Shared Aspirations and Dreams: Talk about and investigate shared dreams and yearnings. Seeing each other's drawn out objectives makes a feeling of solidarity and reason.

Nonverbal Correspondence: Focus on nonverbal prompts. Non-verbal communication, signals, and looks convey feelings that may not be unequivocally communicated in words.

Pardoning and Acknowledgment: Practice absolution and acknowledgment. Accept your partner's flaws and acknowledge your own imperfections to strengthen your emotional connection.

Investigate Each Other's Qualities: Talk about and investigate your singular qualities and convictions. Adjusting your qualities encourages a more profound feeling of association and similarity.

Focus on Close to home Requirements: Recognize

and focus on one another's feelings. Understanding and satisfying these necessities adds to an all the more sincerely satisfying relationship.

Observe Close to home Achievements: Recognize and celebrate profound achievements, whether it's self-improvement, beating difficulties, or extending your close to home association.

Make a Place of refuge: Lay out a safe and without judgment space for open articulation. Both partners are encouraged to share their true selves without fear of criticism when they feel emotionally safe.

Mindfulness as a Team: Practice care together. Emotional awareness can be improved through shared moments of reflection, deep conversations, or meditation.

Be Available in Troublesome Times: Appear for one another during troublesome times. Being available and offering support makes major areas of strength for a for close to home closeness.

Investigate Each Other's Interests: Explore each other's passions and take an interest in them. Understanding what gives pleasure and satisfaction to your accomplice develops your profound association.

By integrating these systems into your relationship, you can encourage a significant profound closeness that improves the general prosperity and life span of your organization.

Understanding Emotional Needs

Understanding and meeting each other's feelings is major for a solid and satisfying relationship. Here are procedures to upgrade how you might interpret profound necessities and how to address them:

Open Exchange: Start transparent discussions about your feelings. Urge your accomplice to share their requirements too. The foundation for mutual understanding is laid by communicating clearly.

Listening intently: Practice undivided attention during conversations about profound requirements. Really focus, pose explaining inquiries, and show compassion to understand your accomplice's sentiments completely.

Self-Reflection: Consider your own feelings. Comprehend what gives you pleasure, security, and a feeling of association. This mindfulness verbalizes your necessities to your accomplice.

Use "I" Explanations: While communicating your feelings, use "I" explanations to try not to sound accusatory. For instance, say, "I feel upheld when..." as opposed to "You never support me."

Focus on Needs: Recognize and focus on the main feelings for both you and your accomplice. Understanding the key components that add to close to home satisfaction takes into consideration designated endeavors.

Make note of nonverbal cues: Pay attention to your partner's nonverbal cues about how they're feeling. Some of the time, feelings are communicated through non-verbal communication, looks, or inconspicuous ways of behaving.

Regular visits: Plan standard registrations to examine how every one of you is feeling inwardly. This continuous discourse encourages a nonstop comprehension of developing requirements.

Empathy: Develop sympathy. Come at the situation from your accomplice's perspective to more readily grasp their profound encounters. Sympathy fabricates an association and fortifies your capacity to address each other's issues.

Get familiar with One another's Ways to express affection: Investigate each other's main avenues for affection, as characterized by Gary Chapman (Uplifting statements, Demonstrations of Administration, Getting Gifts, Quality Time, and Actual Touch). Understanding how your accomplice feels adored can direct your endeavors.

Ask Straightforwardly: Once in a while, the best method for understanding feelings is to straightforwardly inquire. Ask, "What makes you feel loved?" for example. or on the other hand "How might I uphold you inwardly?"

Observe Triumphs: Celebrate each other's achievements, no matter how modest they may be. Emotional well-being and contentment are aided by achievement recognition.

Adjust to Evolving Needs: Perceive that feelings might advance over the long run. Be versatile and open to reevaluating and changing your ways to deal with address evolving issues.

Shared Objectives: Talk about and lay out shared close to home objectives for the relationship. Adjusting your desires makes a typical reason and heading for profound satisfaction.

Keep away from Suppositions: Try not to make suppositions about your accomplice's feelings. All things considered, look for explanation through exchange to guarantee an unmistakable comprehension.

Establish a Supportive Setting: Encourage a strong climate where the two accomplices have a solid sense of reassurance communicating their feelings and necessities unafraid of judgment or analysis.

By proactively taking part in these techniques, you can extend how you might interpret each other's feelings and establish a relationship climate that is strong, satisfying, and genuinely improving.

Expressing Love and Affection

Communicating affection and friendship is imperative for building and supporting areas of strength for an association. Here are systems to really communicate love and warmth in your relationship:

Verbal Confirmations: Use language to convey your love. To reassure your partner of your love, regularly share verbal affirmations, compliments, and affectionate expressions.

Dedicated Time: Focus on quality time together. Spending focused time strengthens your emotional connection, whether it's on a date night, a weekend away, or just doing things together.

Actual Touch: Include physical contact in your everyday interactions. Embraces, kisses, and different types of friendly touch convey warmth and closeness.

Demonstrations of Administration: Perform demonstrations of administration to show your adoration. Little motions, like assisting with errands, preparing a dinner, or aiding undertakings, show your obligation to supporting your accomplice.

Acts of kindness: Participate in acts of kindness. Shock your cooperate with little gifts, notes, or other customized badge of fondness to communicate your affection.

Towards Kindness: Practice arbitrary thoughtful gestures. A loving and positive relationship is made possible by small acts of kindness and generosity.

Offer Thanks: Routinely offer thanks for your accomplice. Recognize their commitments, endeavors, and the positive effect they have on your life.

Make Ceremonies: Make rituals that represent your love. This could incorporate a particular approach to bidding farewell, a normal registration schedule, or whatever other significant custom that reinforces your security.

Compose Love Letters: Compose genuine letters to communicate your affection. A composed statement of your sentiments can be an enduring and significant method for conveying warmth.

Keep in Mind Special Dates: Recollect and celebrate exceptional dates like commemorations, birthday celebrations, and different achievements. Acknowledgment of these events exhibits your care and responsibility.

Plan Shock Dates: Plan shock dates or trips. Unconstrained and startling encounters add a component of energy to the relationship.

Be Mindful: Be mindful of your accomplice's necessities and inclinations. Your emotional connection is strengthened when you demonstrate that you are aware of their desires and considerate of them.

Share Tender Words: Utilize warm affectionate nicknames. Tending to your join forces with cherishing monikers or terms supports the profound connection between you.

Undivided attention: Effectively pay attention to your accomplice. Create an environment that encourages open communication and connection by demonstrating a sincere interest in their thoughts, feelings, and experiences.

Support During Difficulties: Offer unfaltering help during testing times. Being there for your accomplice genuinely encourages a feeling that all is well with the world and love.

Observe Accomplishments: Praise each other's accomplishments and triumphs. Positive aspects of your relationship are bolstered when achievements are acknowledged.

Express Love Through Activities: Allow your activities to express stronger than words. Reliable and smart activities that mirror your affection add to an enduring and significant association.

Accept Unpredictability: Embrace immediacy in communicating love. Engage in unexpected acts of affection with your partner to maintain a dynamic and exciting relationship.

By integrating these systems into your relationship, you can make a rich embroidery of affection and friendship, encouraging a profound and getting through close to home association with your accomplice.

Fostering Emotional Connection

Stimulating Emotional Bonding Stimulating and deepening one's emotional bond is crucial to a happy relationship. Here are systems to reinforce the profound connection between accomplices:

Ordinary Registrations: Plan normal registrations to talk about sentiments, concerns, and encounters. This continuous correspondence guarantees that you stay associated on a close to home level.

Vulnerability Shared: Share weaknesses and uncertainties. Focusing on your feelings of dread and permitting your accomplice to do similar encourages a feeling of closeness and trust.

Compassionate listening: Practice listening with empathy. Put forth a cognizant attempt to figure out your accomplice's viewpoint and feelings, approving their sentiments.

Shared Encounters: Make and offer significant encounters together. Whether it's voyaging, attempting new exercises, or confronting difficulties collectively, shared encounters extend close to home associations.

Manifest Appreciation: Consistently offer thanks for one another. Recognize the positive traits and behaviors that help the relationship thrive.

Make Profound Ceremonies: Lay out profound ceremonies,

like day to day confirmations, week after week reflections, or unique minutes that represent your close to home association.

Steady Signals: Exhibit support through signals. Show up for your accomplice during the two victories and difficulties, exhibiting your obligation to their profound prosperity.

Quality Time: Spend quality time together first. Engage in activities that foster genuine connection and comprehension while avoiding distractions.

Nonverbal Correspondence: Focus on nonverbal prompts. A touch, a grin, or other nonverbal articulations can convey a profundity of feeling that words may not catch.

Profound Discussions: Engage in meaningful, in-depth conversations. Examine your fantasies, values, and the parts of life that are essential to both of you.

Shared Objectives: Lay out shared objectives and goals. Pursuing normal targets makes a feeling of solidarity and reason in the relationship.

Apologize and Excuse: Practice pardoning and apologize when required. Relinquishing feelings of disdain and exhibiting the capacity to pardon reinforces close to home bonds.

Observe Close to home Achievements: Celebrate emotional milestones like personal development, overcoming obstacles, and new levels of intimacy.

Make a Place of refuge: Develop a safe and without judgment space for communicating feelings. Having a good sense of security to share considerations and sentiments improves the profundity of close to home association.

Individual Happiness: Empower and uphold each other's singular prosperity. Perceive that individual satisfaction adds to the general wellbeing of the relationship.

Plan for the future: Talk about and share your dreams for what's in store. An emotional connection that lasts for a long time is strengthened by knowing each other's goals.

Express Warmth: Use physical touch, loving words, and loving gestures to show your affection on a regular basis. These articulations build up the profound connection between accomplices.

Embrace Change Together: Embrace life changes together. Flexibility and common help during changes add to a versatile close to home association.

By reliably carrying out these procedures, couples can cultivate a profound and persevering through close to home association, making a relationship that isn't major areas of strength for just likewise enhanced with common perspective, trust, and closeness.

Chapter 6

Growth and Adaptation

Development and transformation are fundamental parts of a dynamic and advancing relationship. Here are procedures to explore development and change as a team:

Individual Thoughts: Routinely ponder your singular objectives and desires. Understanding self-awareness adds to a more amicable variation as a team.

Open Correspondence: Keep up with open correspondence about private and social development. Examine changes, objectives, and developing needs to guarantee arrangement.

A Common Vision: Lay out a common vision for what's in store. Adjusting your yearnings cultivates a feeling of solidarity and reason, advancing development in a commonly strong climate.

Recognize accomplishments: Celebrate individual and shared accomplishments. Recognizing achievements makes a positive environment and supports the feeling of progress.

Accept Change: Embrace change as a characteristic piece of life. Maintain a collaborative mindset and be able to adapt to changes in the environment.

Shared Help: Deal and look for common help during times of development and change. Being each other's team promoter adds to a strong organization.

Constant Learning: Embrace a mentality of persistent learning. As people and as a couple, flexibility and a readiness to learn add to continuous development.

Modular Planning: Be adaptable in your preparation. Life might unfurl surprisingly, and the capacity to adjust plans advances flexibility and solidarity.

Standard Relationship Registrations: Plan normal relationship registrations to talk about development and variation. Both partners are on the same page as a result of this ongoing conversation.

Put forth New Objectives Together: Occasionally put forth new objectives together. Cooperative objective setting keeps the relationship dynamic and empowers shared accomplishments.

Exploring Changes: Explore life advances together. Managing transitions together builds stronger bonds, whether they involve career shifts, relocations, or other significant shifts.

Empower Self-awareness: Empower and uphold each other's self-improvement. Giving space to individual development adds to a more grounded and seriously satisfying organization.

Embrace Difficulties as Any open doors: View difficulties as any open doors for development. Conquering snags together can prompt a more profound association and a more grounded relationship.

Make relationship health a priority: Focus on the strength of the relationship in the midst of individual development. Guarantee that self-awareness supplements the prosperity of the organization.

Reestablish Responsibility: Renew your commitment to each other on a regular basis. During times of change, reaffirming your commitment fosters a sense of security and continuity.

Make New Practices: Lay out new customs as a team. This makes a feeling of solidness and congruity even as different parts of life might change.

Taking care of oneself Practices: Make self-care routines a priority. Dealing with your singular prosperity adds to the general soundness of the relationship during seasons of development.

Offer Thanks: Offer thanks for the development and positive changes in one another. Positive and supportive relationships are reinforced when progress is acknowledged and appreciated.

By embracing development and transformation with a cooperative and receptive methodology, couples can explore the developing idea of their relationship, encouraging strength, solidarity, and proceeded with individual and social turn of events.

Individual and Collective Growth

Individual and collective growth are essential for the overall well-being and longevity of a relationship. Here are strategies to support both individual and shared growth within a partnership:

Individual Growth: Encourage Personal Goals: Support and encourage each other's personal goals and aspirations. Create an environment where both partners feel empowered to pursue individual growth.

Provide Space for Independence: Recognize the importance of independence. Allow each other the space to explore personal interests, hobbies, and self-discovery.

Communicate Personal Aspirations: Share your individual aspirations and discuss your vision for personal growth. Open communication sets the stage for mutual understanding and support.

Celebrate Individual Achievements: Celebrate each other's individual achievements. Acknowledging personal successes reinforces a positive atmosphere in the relationship.

Prioritize Self-Care: Emphasize the importance of self-care. Encourage activities that promote mental, emotional, and physical well-being for each partner.

Continuous Learning: Foster a mindset of continuous learning. Engage in activities that promote personal development and the acquisition of new skills.

Respect Individual Timelines: Recognize that personal growth occurs at different rates. Respect each other's individual timelines and be patient during periods of self-discovery.

Seek Feedback: Seek constructive feedback from each other. Provide a supportive space for sharing insights and reflections on personal growth journeys.

Set Personal Boundaries: Establish and communicate personal boundaries. Clearly defining individual needs and limits contributes to a healthy balance between independence and togetherness.

Collective Growth:

Define Shared Goals: Collaboratively define shared goals for the relationship. This could include career aspirations, lifestyle choices, or broader visions for the future.

Regular Goal-Setting Sessions: Schedule regular sessions to set and revisit shared goals. This ongoing dialogue ensures that both partners remain aligned in their aspirations.

Encourage Mutual Learning: Encourage learning together. Whether through shared hobbies, educational pursuits, or exploring new experiences, mutual learning strengthens the bond.

Navigate Challenges Together: Approach challenges as a team. Collaborate to find solutions and face difficulties together, fostering a sense of unity and resilience.

Create a Shared Vision: Establish a shared vision for the relationship. Discuss and visualize the kind of partnership you both aspire to create over time.

Celebrate Relationship Milestones: Acknowledge and celebrate relationship milestones. Whether it's anniversaries or other significant moments, recognizing shared achievements reinforces commitment.

Adaptability as a Couple: Develop adaptability as a couple. Recognize that circumstances may change, and the ability to adapt together contributes to the relationship's longevity.

Encourage Mutual Support: Provide unwavering support for each other's endeavors. Being each other's cheerleader creates a positive and encouraging environment for collective growth.

Regular Relationship Check-Ins: Schedule regular check-ins to assess the state of the relationship. These discussions provide an opportunity to address any misalignments in individual or shared growth.

Celebrate Each Other's Growth: Celebrate not only individual achievements but also each other's growth within the relationship. Acknowledge the positive changes and development you see in your partner.

By prioritizing both individual and collective growth, couples can create a relationship that not only supports personal fulfillment but also flourishes as a dynamic and evolving partnership.

Adapting to Changes

Adapting to changes is a crucial skill for a resilient and thriving relationship. Here are strategies to navigate and adapt to changes together:

Open Communication: Maintain open and honest communication. Discuss any changes, whether they are external circumstances or internal shifts within the relationship.

Express Feelings: Encourage each other to express feelings about the changes. Create a safe space for sharing concerns, fears, or excitement related to the evolving circumstances.

Embrace Flexibility: Cultivate a flexible mindset. Understand that change is a natural part of life, and being adaptable as a couple fosters resilience.

Collaborative Decision-Making: Make decisions collaboratively. Involve both partners in discussions and decision-making processes related to changes, ensuring a sense of shared responsibility.

Set Realistic Expectations: Establish realistic expectations about the changes. Acknowledge potential challenges and discuss how you can navigate them together.

Seek Mutual Understanding: Strive to understand each other's perspectives on the changes. Mutual understanding promotes empathy and strengthens the bond during transitions.

Develop Coping Strategies: Together, develop coping strategies for dealing with the stress or uncertainties that may accompany changes. Having a plan can provide a sense of stability.

Maintain Emotional Support: Offer emotional support to each other. Recognize that transitions can be emotionally challenging, and being there for your partner contributes to a strong foundation.

Celebrate New Opportunities: Embrace the positive aspects of change. Celebrate new opportunities, growth, and the potential for positive developments that may arise.

Adapt Routines: Be willing to adapt routines and habits. Changes often require adjustments to daily life, and a collaborative approach to adapting routines can ease the transition.

Learn and Grow Together: View changes as opportunities for mutual learning and growth. Embrace the journey of evolving together as a couple.

Establish a Plan: If the changes are significant, establish a plan together. Outline the steps you'll take, roles you'll play, and any support systems you can rely on during the transition.

Maintain a Sense of Humor: Infuse a sense of humor into the process. Laughter can be a powerful tool for navigating challenges and maintaining a positive outlook.

Prioritize Self-Care: Emphasize self-care for both partners. Taking care of your individual well-being contributes to the overall health of the relationship during times of change.

Lean on Each Other: Lean on each other for support. Knowing that you have a reliable partner to navigate changes with can provide comfort and assurance.

Celebrate Adaptability: Acknowledge and celebrate your adaptability as a couple. Recognize the strength you possess in facing changes together.

Seek Professional Guidance: If needed, consider seeking professional guidance. Relationship counselors or therapists can provide valuable insights and tools to navigate changes effectively.

Reevaluate and Adjust: Periodically reevaluate the impact of changes on the relationship. Adjust strategies and plans as needed to ensure continued alignment and harmony.

By approaching changes with a collaborative and supportive mindset, couples can not only adapt successfully but also use these moments as opportunities for growth and deepening their connection.

Setting Future Goals Together

Setting future goals together is a powerful way to strengthen your relationship and create a shared vision for the future. Here are strategies to collaboratively set and pursue future goals:

Initiate Open Discussions: Start open discussions about your individual aspirations and visions for the future. Encourage each other to express long-term goals and dreams.

Identify Shared Values: Identify shared values that will guide your future goals. Understanding your core values as a couple ensures that your goals align with what matters most to both of you.

Establish Short-Term and Long-Term Goals: Outline both short-term and long-term goals. Short-term goals provide immediate direction, while long-term goals create a vision for the future.

Prioritize Goals Together: Prioritize your goals collectively. Discuss which goals are most important to both of you and agree on their significance in shaping your shared future.

Create a Vision Board: Develop a vision board together. This visual representation of your goals can serve as a constant reminder of the future you are working towards as a couple.

Break Down Goals into Steps: Break down larger goals into smaller, manageable steps. This makes the journey more achievable and allows for incremental progress.

Establish Timelines: Set realistic timelines for achieving your goals. Clearly defined timelines provide structure and help you track your progress over time.

Assign Responsibilities: Assign responsibilities for each goal. Clearly defining roles ensures that both partners actively contribute to the pursuit of your shared aspirations.

Regularly Reassess Goals: Schedule regular check-ins to reassess your goals. Life circumstances may change, and your goals may need adjustment to remain relevant and achievable.

Celebrate Milestones: Celebrate milestones along the way. Acknowledge and celebrate the progress you make toward your goals, reinforcing a positive and supportive atmosphere.

Adaptability to Changing Circumstances: Cultivate adaptability. Recognize that unexpected changes may occur, and being flexible in your approach to achieving goals ensures resilience.

Support Each Other's Individual Goals: In addition to shared goals, support each other's individual goals. Encourage personal growth and celebrate individual achievements.

Explore Shared Interests: Identify shared interests and incorporate them into your future plans. Pursuing common passions strengthens your connection and adds joy to your journey.

Seek Professional Advice: If your goals involve complex financial or career decisions, consider seeking professional advice. Financial planners or career counselors can provide valuable insights.

Create a Financial Plan: If applicable, create a financial plan to support your goals. This includes budgeting, saving, and making informed decisions about financial aspects of your future.

Regularly Communicate Progress: Maintain open communication about your progress. Regularly discuss how you're both feeling about your goals, and address any challenges that arise.

Revisit and Refine Goals: Periodically revisit and refine your goals. As your relationship evolves, your aspirations may change, and adjusting your goals accordingly ensures continued alignment.

Celebrate Goal Achievement: Celebrate the achievement of significant goals. Whether it's a small victory or a major milestone, taking time to celebrate reinforces your shared accomplishments.

By actively engaging in these strategies, you and your partner can create a future that reflects your shared aspirations, strengthens your bond, and provides a roadmap for a fulfilling life together.

Chapter 7
Relationship Wellness

Relationship wellness is crucial for maintaining a healthy and fulfilling partnership. Here are strategies to promote overall well-being in your relationship:

Regular Check-Ins: Schedule regular check-ins to assess the health of your relationship. These discussions provide an opportunity to address concerns, express feelings, and ensure ongoing alignment.

Prioritize Quality Time: Prioritize quality time together. Whether it's date nights, shared activities, or simply spending time connecting, quality moments strengthen the bond between partners.

Effective Communication: Cultivate effective communication skills. Listen actively, express thoughts and feelings clearly, and be attentive to each other's needs.

Mutual Respect: Uphold mutual respect. Treat your partner with kindness, consideration, and acknowledgment of their individuality.

Nurture Emotional Intimacy: Continuously nurture emotional intimacy. Share vulnerabilities, engage in deep conversations, and foster a sense of closeness.

Express Love and Affection: Regularly express love and affection. Verbal affirmations, physical touch, and gestures of love contribute to a positive relationship atmosphere.

Practice Gratitude: Cultivate a practice of gratitude. Regularly express appreciation for each other, focusing on the positive aspects of your relationship.

Balanced Independence: Find a balance between independence and togetherness. Allow each other space for personal growth while maintaining a strong connection as a couple.

Shared Responsibilities: Share responsibilities in the relationship. Collaborative efforts in daily tasks contribute to a sense of partnership and equality.

Embrace Fun and Playfulness: Embrace fun and playfulness. Inject laughter and joy into your relationship by engaging in activities that bring happiness to both of you.

Establish Rituals: Establish meaningful rituals. Whether it's a morning routine, shared hobbies, or special traditions, rituals create a sense of stability and connection.

Conflict Resolution Skills: Develop effective conflict resolution skills. Learn to address disagreements constructively, finding solutions that strengthen rather than harm the relationship.

Encourage Individual Growth: Support each other's individual growth. Encourage personal development, and celebrate achievements that contribute to individual well-being.

Foster Trust: Prioritize trust in the relationship. Trust forms the foundation for a secure and lasting connection between partners.

Practice Active Listening: Practice active listening. Show genuine interest in your partner's thoughts and feelings, fostering a deeper understanding.

Maintain Intimacy: Sustain physical and emotional

intimacy. Regularly engage in activities that strengthen both the emotional and physical aspects of your connection.

Set Boundaries: Establish and respect boundaries. Clearly communicate your needs and limits to ensure a healthy and respectful relationship dynamic.

Seek Support if Needed: If challenges arise, be open to seeking support. Relationship counseling or therapy can provide valuable tools for overcoming obstacles and strengthening your connection.

By incorporating these strategies into your relationship, you can foster a holistic sense of well-being, ensuring that your partnership remains strong, fulfilling, and resilient over time.

Mental and Physical Health in Relationships

Keeping up with mental and actual wellbeing is fundamental for the prosperity of people and the soundness of a relationship.

Here are techniques to focus on mental and actual wellbeing inside an organization:

Supportive Networks: Open Discourse About Emotional wellness Make a place of refuge for open exchange about psychological well-being. Support legit discussions about sentiments, stressors, and close to home prosperity.

A supportive setting: Cultivate a strong climate for one another's psychological well-being. Be understanding during testing times, and proposition support and compassion.

Seek Expert Assistance: If necessary, empower looking for proficient assistance. A psychological well-being proficient can give direction and backing in overseeing psychological wellness challenges.

Teach Yourselves: Teach yourselves about psychological well-being. Understanding normal psychological wellness conditions lessens disgrace and advances compassion.

Focus on Taking care of oneself: Focus on taking care of oneself practices. Urge each other to participate in exercises that advance mental prosperity, like care, unwinding, or leisure activities.

Lay out Solid Survival techniques: Collaborate to develop healthy strategies for overcoming challenges and stress. This could incorporate activity, reflection, or different systems that help mental versatility.

Standard Registrations: Make regular mental health check-ins a priority. Talk about how you're feeling, any stressors you might be confronting, and team up on ways of supporting one another.

Care Practices: Integrate care rehearses into your everyday practice. Care can improve profound mindfulness and add to by and large mental prosperity.

Observe Emotional well-being Accomplishments: Celebrate accomplishments connected with psychological wellness. Recognize and value endeavors to keep up with and work on mental prosperity.

Physical fitness: Make regular exercise a priority: Focus on normal activity together. Whether it's taking strolls, working out, or participating in proactive tasks, practice adds to actual prosperity.

Energize Good dieting Propensities: Support each other in keeping up with good dieting propensities. Plan and get ready nutritious feasts together to advance in general actual wellbeing.

Get Normal Check-Ups: Go to normal wellbeing check-ups. Observing actual wellbeing through normal clinical check-ups can recognize potential issues almost immediately.

Quality Rest: Focus on quality rest. Lay out sound rest schedules to guarantee the two accomplices get satisfactory rest for ideal physical and mental prosperity.

Hydration: Support legitimate hydration. It is essential for overall health to drink enough water, which can improve energy levels and cognitive function.

Limit Substance Use: Be aware of substance use. Restricting or staying away from unnecessary liquor or substance utilization adds to actual prosperity.

Joint Wellbeing Exercises: Take part in joint wellbeing exercises. Whether it's climbing, trekking, or partaking in sports together, shared proactive tasks advance a solid way of life.

Stress The board Procedures: Learn and rehearse pressure the executives methods. This might incorporate profound breathing, reflection, or different techniques to lighten physical and mental strain.

Energize Standard Breaks: Support each other in enjoying normal reprieves.

Whether it's short strolls during the business day or arranged excursions, breaks add to generally speaking prosperity.

Solid Sexual Closeness: Keep a sound sexual relationship. Open correspondence about wants and inclinations cultivates a positive actual association between accomplices.

Stop Unfortunate Propensities Together: If relevant, quit undesirable propensities together. Whether it's smoking or other adverse ways of behaving, support each other in making positive way of life changes.

Take a look at new forms of exercise: Persistently investigate new proactive tasks. Attempting new things together keeps actual health drawing in and pleasant.

Make a Health Plan: Cooperatively make a wellbeing plan. Describe the steps you will take together to achieve and maintain your physical well-being, as well as your health goals.

Celebrate milestones in health: Celebrate wellbeing achievements. Whether it's arriving at a wellness objective or rolling out sure improvements, recognizing accomplishments supports a guarantee to actual wellbeing.

By effectively integrating these procedures into your relationship, you can cultivate a climate that focuses on both mental and actual wellbeing, adding to the general prosperity and essentialness of your association.

Supportive Networks

Supportive Networks A healthy relationship depends on creating and maintaining supportive networks. Here are procedures to develop strong organizations inside your association:

Open Correspondence About Friendly Associations: Cultivate open correspondence about friendly associations. Examine the significance of having strong organizations and offer your singular inclinations for mingling.

Shared Regard for Social Limits: Regard each other's social limits. Comprehend and recognize the requirement for individual space and associations outside the relationship.

Support Fellowships: Urge each other to keep up with and sustain fellowships. Perceive the worth of assorted social associations for self-awareness and prosperity.

Partake in Friendly Exercises

Together: Participate in friendly exercises as a team. Whether it's going to occasions, gatherings, or get-togethers, shared encounters add to major areas of strength for an organization.

Recognize One Another's Social

Successes: Recognize one another's social accomplishments. Recognize and value the positive connections and associations that add to your accomplice's prosperity.

Be Steady of Family Ties: Support each other's

associations with relatives. Provide emotional support during family interactions and acknowledge the significance of family connections.

Go to Get-togethers Together: Go to get-togethers together whenever the situation allows. A sense of integration and shared experiences are created when people participate in each other's social circles.

Offer Consistent encouragement During Difficulties: Show up for one another during social difficulties. Offer basic encouragement and direction while exploring complex social circumstances or clashes.

Establish Social Networks for Others: Foster shared interpersonal organizations. Develop associations with different couples or gatherings of companions, making a steady local area that upgrades your relationship.

Offset Time with Companions and Accomplice: Figure out a

harmony between opportunity invested with companions and energy gave to your relationship. Focus on quality time together while likewise sustaining individual social associations.

Take part in Friendly Clubs or Exercises: Investigate social clubs or exercises together. Joining bunches lined up with shared interests gives open doors to both individual and joint social commitment.

Regard Protection: Regard each other's requirement for protection in friendly associations. Keep up with trust by recognizing and regarding individual limits.

Empower Inclusivity: Support inclusivity in groups of friends. Really try to incorporate each other in your separate social exercises, encouraging a feeling of shared contribution.

Share Social Objectives: Talk about and share social objectives. Align your goals for social connections, whether they're expanding your social circle, attending more events, or reuniting with old friends.

Support During Social Difficulties: Offer help during social difficulties or clashes. Resolving issues together reinforces the relationship and gives an establishment to exploring future social circumstances.

Support of a high quality in trying times: Offer quality help during troublesome times. Being there for your partner demonstrates your commitment, and social networks play a crucial role in assisting people in overcoming obstacles.

Recognize Social Success: Celebrate social achievements together. Whether it's a companion's accomplishment or a fruitful get-together, partaking in one another's delights reinforces the connection between accomplices.

If necessary, seek professional

advice: Consider consulting a professional for guidance if you encounter difficulties managing social connections. Counselors or therapists in relationships can offer insight and strategies for navigating social dynamics.

You can build a supportive network that improves the well-being of both partners and strengthens the overall foundation of your partnership by actively incorporating these strategies into your relationship.

Sustaining a Healthy Relationship Over Time

Supporting a sound relationship over the long run requires continuous exertion and responsibility. Here are techniques to encourage life span and prosperity in your organization:

Focus on Correspondence: Keep up with transparent correspondence. Make it a habit to check in on each other on a regular basis to share feelings, thoughts, and experiences and build a strong bond.

Develop Common Regard: Maintain shared regard. Treat each other with generosity, thought, and appreciation for your singular characteristics and commitments.

Sustain Close to home Closeness: Constantly sustain profound closeness. Engage in activities that strengthen your emotional connection, show love, and share your vulnerabilities.

Versatility to Change: Develop versatility. Recognize that the two people and connections advance over the long haul, and embrace changes together.

Spending Time Together Focus on quality time. Devote minutes for shared exercises, significant discussions, and making enduring recollections.

Customary Relationship Registrations: Plan ordinary relationship registrations. Examine the situation in your relationship, talk about your goals, and address any issues or difficulties that may arise.

Keep up with Trust: Focus on trust. Be dependable, straightforward, and genuine, building up an underpinning of trust that is fundamental for a solid and enduring relationship.

Observe Achievements: Celebrate milestones in your relationship. Recognize commemorations, accomplishments, and minutes that mark the excursion you've shared together.

Proceed with Individual Development: Empower and uphold each other's singular development. Perceive that self-improvement adds to the general soundness of the relationship.

Develop Shared Interests: Investigate and develop shared interests. Partaking in exercises you both appreciate fortifies your bond and gives pleasure to the relationship.

Learn to forgive: Embrace absolution. Relinquish past complaints, address clashes valuably, and center around building a positive future together.

Make and Keep up with Ceremonies: Lay out and keep up with relationship ceremonies. Rituals contribute to stability, whether it's a weekly date night, a special tradition, or daily love expressions.

Respect the Space of Others: Respect one another's need for privacy. Offsetting freedom with harmony is fundamental for a solid dynamic.

Support Sentiment: Keep sentiment alive. Shock each other with signals, express friendship, and track down imaginative ways of keeping up with the flash in your relationship.

Weather conditions Difficulties Together: Face difficulties collectively. Supporting each other during troublesome times reinforces the strength of your relationship.

Value One another: Routinely express appreciation. Recognize and esteem each other's endeavors, characteristics, and the positive effect you have on one another's lives.

Ceaseless Learning: Develop a mentality of nonstop learning. Be curious about the changing preferences, goals, and desires of the other.

Look for Proficient Direction if necessary: In the event that diligent difficulties emerge, think about looking for proficient direction. Counselors and therapists in relationships can provide helpful insights and strategies for overcoming difficult challenges.

By reliably carrying out these systems, you can sustain a relationship that gets through everyday hardship as well as keeps on thriving, giving satisfaction and joy to the two accomplices.

All in all, encouraging a solid and getting through relationship requires devotion, correspondence, and a common obligation to development. By focusing on viable correspondence, building trust, sustaining profound closeness, and supporting each other's individual and aggregate objectives, couples can make an establishment for a solid and tough organization.

The excursion includes exploring difficulties, adjusting to change, and effectively keeping up with the prosperity of the two people. Developing a steady organization and supporting a good arrangement among freedom and harmony further add to the life span of the relationship.

Keep in mind that making an ongoing effort, comprehending the milestones that come along the way, and celebrating those milestones are crucial to developing a relationship that is both satisfying and enduring as you embark on this journey together. May your relationship be a wellspring of satisfaction, backing, and development for the two accomplices.

Recap of Key Points

A. Certainly, a Summary of the Key Points Key points from the Ultimate Couples Guide to a Healthy Relationship can be summarized as follows:

I.   Presentation: Investigated the significance of an exhaustive aide for couples looking for a solid relationship.

A. Motivation behind the Aide: Framed the aide's level headed to give bits of knowledge and techniques to couples to construct and keep major areas of strength for a, relationship.

B. The Value of Strong Relationships: Accentuated the meaning of solid connections for individual prosperity, bliss, and generally speaking life fulfillment.

II. Relational abilities:
Focused on the pivotal job of compelling correspondence in cultivating understanding and association.

A. Powerful Correspondence Methods: Investigated systems for clear and compassionate correspondence, including undivided attention and offering viewpoints and sentiments transparently.

B. Undivided attention:emphasized the significance of active listening for improving communication and comprehension.

C. Compromise Procedures: Examined productive ways to deal with settling clashes, advancing an agreeable relationship.

Building Trust: Investigated the underpinning of trust and procedures to upgrade and keep up with.